BRIEF **BB** BOOKS

THE BOOK OF BOOKS

A short guide to reading the Bible

GEOFF ROBSON

matthiasmedia

SYDNEY · YOUNGSTOWN

The Book of Books
© Geoff Robson 2015

Matthias Media
(St Matthias Press Ltd ACN 067 558 365)
Email: info@matthiasmedia.com.au
Internet: www.matthiasmedia.com.au
Please visit our website for current postal and telephone
contact information.

Matthias Media (USA)
Email: sales@matthiasmedia.com
Internet: www.matthiasmedia.com
Please visit our website for current postal and telephone
contact information.

ISBN 978 1 922206 82 4

Cover design and typesetting by affiniT Design.

CONTENTS

1. THE BOOK THAT CHANGES LIVES

Gaylord Kambarami, the former General Secretary of the Bible Society of Zimbabwe, once offered a man a copy of the New Testament. But this man wasn't interested, and assured Kambarami he'd only use the pages of the Bible to roll cigarettes. "I will make a deal with you", Kambarami replied. "I will give you this book if you promise to read every page before you smoke it." He handed over the New Testament and hoped for the best, and the men parted ways.

More than a decade later, Kambarami was attending a conference when, to his surprise, the speaker on the platform suddenly pointed him out to the audience. "This man doesn't remember me, but I remember him", the speaker said. "About 15 years ago he tried to sell me a New Testament. When I refused to buy it he gave it to me, even though I told him I would use the pages to roll cigarettes. He made me promise to read the pages before I smoked them. Well, I smoked Matthew. I smoked Mark. Then I smoked Luke. But when I got to John 3:16, I couldn't smoke any more! My life was changed from that moment!" This man, like countless millions before and after him, had been captured by the message of the Bible. He became a Christian, and devoted his life to spreading the good news of Jesus Christ that he had first encountered in the pages of that New Testament.[1]

That incredible story offers a tiny glimpse into the power of the Bible. By any measure, it is a book like no other. Well over six billion copies have been printed worldwide, and it continues to top global bestseller lists every year.[2] Wycliffe Bible Translators estimate that at least a portion of the Bible has

---

1   This story is recounted in HJ Sala, *Why You Can Have Confidence in the Bible: Bridging the Distance Between Your Heart and God's Word*, Harvest House, Eugene, 2008, pp. 203-4.

2   The only possible exception is 2007, when the final *Harry Potter* book sold 44 million copies.

I He was convicted by the Holy Spirit.

been translated into <u>2883 languages,</u>[3] and Gideons International (a Bible distribution ministry) has given away more than two billion copies of the good book on its own. A single printing press in Nanjing, China, produces <u>12 million Bibles annually</u>—that's 23 Bibles per minute, every single minute of the year.

Of course, facts and figures alone don't tell the whole story, and the Bible's impact goes way beyond mere statistics. Its influence on modern Western culture, for example, is incalculable. In *The Book That Made Your World: How the Bible Created the Soul of Western Civilization,* Indian philosopher and theologian Vishal Mangalwadi offers a sweeping account of the differences between the history and culture of his home nation, and the history and culture of Western society. Mangalwadi chronicles countless ways in which the Bible has positively shaped the Western world's attitudes in such diverse areas as education, technology, service, science, money, language, compassion and freedom. He concludes: "The Bible is not merely a handbook of private piety. It is <u>the very foundation</u>[2] of Western

---

3 Wycliffe Bible Translators, *Our Vision*, Wycliffe UK Ltd, High Wycombe, 2015 (viewed 7 August 2015): http://wycliffe.org.uk/wycliffe/about/vision.html.

2. The Bible should be 'the very foundation' of our lives

civilization."[4] Even a towering figure like Mahatma Gandhi—a man who was fascinated by Jesus Christ yet never became a Christian—recognized the Bible's uniqueness. Speaking to a group of missionaries, he is said to have remarked: "You Christians look after a document containing enough dynamite to blow all civilization to pieces, turn the world upside down and bring peace to a battle-torn planet".

In short, the Bible is far and away the most printed, the most sold, the most given away, the most read, and the most influential book in history.

But times have changed. Our world and our attitudes have changed. Clearly, the Bible is not treated with the same reverence and respect that it once was. Some see this as a positive development—the shedding of old-fashioned cultural baggage and antiquated thinking. Many people find it painfully easy to dismiss the Bible out of hand, like the young woman I recently met on a university campus. When I asked whether she had read the Bible for herself as an adult, this woman—who clearly regarded herself as an enlightened, educated person—replied

---

4 V Mangalwadi, *The Book That Made Your World: How the Bible Created the Soul of Western Civilization*, Thomas Nelson, Nashville, 2011, p. 387.

(without any hint of irony), "No, but a friend of mine read some of it, and she told me it's stupid". For her, that was reason enough to ignore it entirely.

Others, meanwhile, lament the Bible's waning influence and hope to see its message delivered afresh to a new generation. They recognize countless ways in which it has transformed their own life, and they long to see others experience something similar (maybe that's why you've been given this book).

But whatever we make of our history or the changes happening around us, one thing is clear: the mind-boggling statistics and unrivalled cultural impact remind us that the Bible can't be easily ignored.

Yet all this is only part of the story. For the Bible boasts much more than impressive statistics and cultural importance. At its core, the Bible is an intensely personal book,[3] reaching off the page to make the biggest possible claims about the purpose and meaning of our own lives.

If we approach the Bible simply as a kind of cultural artifact, we're in danger of missing the heart of its message and stripping away its greatest power. For the Bible boldly claims to unveil the heart of the human condition and the very meaning of life. It claims to introduce us to the God who made us and

3. The Bible talks directly to you and hopefully has you repent.

who is at the heart of the universe. In fact, it claims to be a direct message of self-revelation *from* the God who made us, and who longs to relate to us personally.

In a sense, reading the Bible is not for the faint-hearted. You don't exactly curl up in your favourite armchair with a Bible and a cup of tea for some nice, restful escapism. It's a challenging, sometimes confronting book. And of course, as a book that has come to us from very different times and places, reading it requires some patience and effort—maybe even some guidance and input from a trusted friend.

Yet when it comes to the Bible, the effort we put in will be repaid many, many times over. As countless millions of individuals (not to mention entire societies) can testify, this book changes lives for the better. Reading it, heeding its message, and following it may do more to impact you and your world than you could imagine, just as it did for Gaylord Kambarami's smoking friend. To put it another way: as you read the Bible for yourself, you may just find that the Bible reads you.

Why? Why has the Bible transformed so many lives and had such a far-reaching, deep impact? What is it actually all about, and what makes this book so special?

1. THE BOOK THAT CHANGES LIVES

Before we address those questions directly, let's clear the ground and get ourselves oriented with some basics.

2. THE BOOK OF BOOKS

The word 'Bible' simply means 'book'. It is, quite literally, *the book*. But a quick flick through its pages will tell you that 'the book' is actually a collection of books. To be more precise, it's a collection of 66 documents, ranging in length from one page through to small books in their own right. These 66 documents were written over a period of around 1,500 years by around 40 different authors, who wrote in Hebrew (almost all of the Old Testament), Aramaic (a very short section of the Old Testament), and Greek (the entire New Testament). The Bibles we read today are based on careful translations of the original Hebrew, Aramaic and Greek texts. To make it easier to navigate our way around the Bible, divisions known as chapters (the big numbers) and verses (the small numbers) have been added to each book over the years. So, for example, John 3:16 means the book of John, chapter 3, verse 16.[5]

The Bible's 66 documents are written in a variety of genres, including poetry, historical narrative, prophecy, law, letters, historical biography, and the vivid imagery and symbolism of what's called 'apocalyptic literature'. So reading and understanding the Bible properly means paying attention to what genre you're reading. Think of a newspaper– hopefully you don't read the comics or the horoscopes in the same way that you read the front page! In a similar way, you don't read biblical poetry in the same way that you read biblical history, law or a biography.

The books of the Bible are arranged roughly (though not precisely) in chronological order, and are

---

5   While chapters and verses are really helpful for navigating the Bible (imagine finding your way around without them!), they carry with them a possible danger: readers sometimes get the impression that each verse stands alone and (if you're lucky) contains an isolated nugget of wisdom or insight. However, it's important to remember that each verse is just like a sentence in most other books we might read–so in order to properly understand what it means, you need to know what comes before it and what comes after it. It's why 'context' is such a buzz word among Christians. It's also worth noting that, just like chapters and verses, the subheadings and paragraph breaks in our modern Bibles were added later and aren't part of the original text.

separated into two sections, or 'testaments'. Thirty-nine of these documents form the Old Testament, which tells the story of the creation of the world, and of God's dealings with humanity prior to the coming of Jesus Christ. In particular, the Old Testament focuses on the history of the ancient nation of Israel across many hundreds of years. The second section, the New Testament, contains 27 documents. These documents provide the historical record of the life, death and resurrection of Jesus Christ (which happened around 2,000 years ago), as well as the birth of Christianity in the decades immediately following Jesus' resurrection from death.

While there is a time gap of around 450 years between the close of the Old Testament and the beginning of the New, these two sections are intimately connected. In fact, it's best to think of the whole Bible as one unfolding story centred on the man Jesus Christ. We'll see more of that in a moment, but for now it's worth noting that the Bible, unlike some other 'holy books', is not simply a collection of ancient wisdom or religious philosophies. It is a collection of historical documents, describing real events in real times and places, and helping us to see the significance and meaning of these events.

So what are those events, and why are they significant for us?

It's possible that before you'll feel ready to consider those questions, you'll want to look at some of the background issues. You might be asking questions like: How do we know that the Bible can be trusted? *Can* we know? Is there any way to be sure that the Bible's claims are reliable and meaningful, or is reading this book just one giant leap of 'blind faith'? Is the Bible even worth reading?

If those are your questions, and you know you'll struggle to listen to the Bible until they're answered, now is a good time to turn ahead to appendix A, 'Why bother with the Bible?' The very short answer is that, thankfully, when it comes to the Bible, we find ourselves on the firmest possible historical ground. You can read your Bible with the highest level of confidence that it's an accurate, reliable record of what really happened. You can also be confident that it contains a message of vital interest to every reader.

But maybe you're ready to simply dive in and get started on the Bible itself, happy to leave the historical questions until later. If that's you, let's keep moving by getting a quick bird's-eye view of what the whole Bible is about.

3. WHAT'S IT ALL ABOUT?

The heart of the Bible's message can be summed up in one word: Jesus. It could also be summed up in a few more words: the life, death, resurrection and promised return of Jesus Christ—the Saviour and King sent into the world by God himself. The 66 books of the Bible come together to give us one big, sweeping story that leads up to, and then flows out of, the coming of Jesus. Once you become familiar with the Bible, you'll start to see the centrality of Jesus everywhere.

For now, that may be all you want to know to get started. If you're ready to let the Bible speak for itself—and you don't want me to spoil the story for you—why not jump ahead to the reading plan (see 'With a plan' in chapter 4, along with appendix C) and go for it? Perhaps you could read the book of Mark, then come back and work through this overview after you've had a taste of the Bible for yourself.

However, if you're just starting out or perhaps you've never read the Bible before, hearing that the whole thing is about Jesus might not mean very much. Or maybe you're still feeling a bit overwhelmed by the size and scope of this massive book. So for those who want more of an overview, let's trace out the stages in the Bible's story to see how each part contributes to the unfolding plot, and to get our heads around where Jesus fits in and why he's so important.[6]

Creation (Genesis 1-2): The Bible starts at the very beginning–literally–with the one and only God creating the entire universe. God made the world and everything in it, including humans, who were made in God's image. As the Creator, God is the ruler

---

6 This outline is based on material in *The Bible Overview* Leader's Manual, written by M Brain, MA Malcolm, MR Malcolm and G Clarke (Matthias Media, Kingsford, 2001). The same material can be found in XV: *The Bible in* 15, an iOS Bible overview app that provides more information, questions, and Bible readings to assist with personal study. You can download it for free at http://matthiasmedia.com/bibleoverview/. The Bible passages provided for each stage aren't intended to be exhaustive (since each idea is explained in multiple parts of the Bible), but should be enough to give you a taste of what the Bible says about each stage of God's unfolding plans.

3. WHAT'S IT ALL ABOUT?

of the entire creation, and yet he gave Adam and Eve (the first people) the privilege of being rulers over his world (under him, of course).

The Bible's account of creation shows that God is the ultimate being and the source of everything, including life itself. This means that to function properly, everyone and everything needs to be understood in relation to him. It also shows that God is infinitely powerful, creating everything simply with a word. Maybe most of all, creation shows that God is gracious and good. He created a world that, at least initially, contained nothing bad. The world was full of delights, and humanity was created to live in loving relationships with God and with each other, even ruling the world under God.

Sounds wonderful, right? Positively idyllic. But it's hardly the world we live in today...

The fall (Genesis 3): Instead of living happily and thankfully in the paradise that God provided, Adam and Eve chose to reject God as their ruler. Rather than listening to God, they ignored him and rejected him. This act of cosmic treason is what the Bible calls 'sin', and it's a disease that has infected the human race and been replicated by each one of us in various ways ever since. This is why sin is such a big deal— it's not just about 'being naughty' or breaking some rules. Sin is fundamentally an attitude that says, "Thanks for creating us, God, but we'll take it from here. We don't need you. We know better than you, and we can decide what's best on our own."

The effects of sin were (and are) devastating. God withdrew his perfect blessing from Adam and Eve, and from all creation. As a result we don't relate rightly to God, our relationships with each other are broken, and we live in a world that experiences the decaying effects of sin. And at death, we face the prospect of being eternally separated from God's goodness. This sounds horrific, but the reality of God's judgement shouldn't come as a surprise. After all, God wouldn't become more moral or more appealing if he responded to human rebellion by saying, "I don't really care how you treat me. Do what you want, and run my world however you choose."

But despite his judgement, God was gracious and he did not give up on humanity.

The pledge (Genesis 12): Even though humans sinned, this was not the end of the story. Throughout the rest of the Bible, we see God at work to save his rebellious world and to establish his kingdom by choosing a human to rule rightly under him. The Bible is ultimately a story of redemption and salvation, which come from the God who redeems and saves.

The story of salvation began when God chose one man, Abraham, and made a pledge (also called a 'covenant'). God committed himself to a special relationship with Abraham, promising that he would make a great nation from Abraham's descendants, and that he would give them a land of their own. He did this so that, in the end, the whole world would be blessed, and humanity's rejection of God would not go on forever.

God's pledge to Abraham shows that God is loving, generous and merciful. While humanity shakes its fist in God's face, God commits himself to bringing blessing to humanity. The pledge also sets up one of the Bible's big themes by showing that God makes and keeps promises. He is faithful, even when we are unfaithful.

Exodus from slavery (Exodus 3 and 19): As Abraham's descendants grew in number, they became known as the nation of Israel. They went to Egypt, and there they were made to be slaves for about 400 years. But

God had not forgotten his pledge to Abraham. He continued to see the nation of Israel as his special people, and he saved them out of slavery in Egypt. The 'Exodus', as that event has become known, was a defining moment in the history of Israel as a nation. While Moses was the human leader of Israel during this time, it's clear that God was the one who redeemed and saved his people.

The Exodus is a great example of how the Bible finds its ultimate meaning and fulfilment in Jesus. The idea of 'freedom from slavery' powerfully captures the truth of what Jesus achieved for us in his death and resurrection. But our slavery was not to a cruel and oppressive human tyrant like Egypt's Pharaoh (as terrible as that was). Our slavery was to something much worse: sin and death. When Jesus died in our place and rose again (as we'll see in a moment), he liberated us from our slavery to death and sin.

The promised land (Exodus 34:10-14 and Joshua 1-6): After bringing Israel out of Egypt, God didn't just leave his people languishing in the desert. Instead, he brought them to the land he had pledged to Abraham and his descendants hundreds of years earlier. Once they arrived in this land, they were meant to live as

God's special people—distinct from the world around them, yet not indifferent to the welfare of other nations, as they were to show God's goodness and righteousness by living out their special relationship with him.

The law (Exodus 20 and Deuteronomy 6): On their way to the promised land, the people of Israel were given instructions on how to live. These instructions told them about what it meant to be in a special relationship with God, and how they could best reflect God's character to the nations around them. The law itself didn't save them (God had already done that when he brought them out of Egypt), but it told them how to live as God's saved people and showed how they could be a blessing to the whole world. The most famous part of the Old Testament law is the Ten Commandments.

The law shows that God is perfectly righteous, or 'holy'. He saves people so they can live his way, under his rule, in a right relationship with him. But the law also shows that God is a loving God, because he allows rebels to relate to him in this way, and he tells them clearly how they can flourish as his people.

Kings (2 Samuel 7): After they had been in the land for some time, God gave Israel kings to rule over it. The king's role was to be God's representative on earth by ruling Israel justly and saving the nation in battle. The king also represented the people before God. The most famous king was David, who was followed by his son, Solomon.

The rule of Israel's kings points us forward to Jesus, the direct descendant of King David, who preached the coming of 'the kingdom of God'. Jesus was a humble servant who (unlike any of Israel's other kings) was perfectly obedient to God, even to the point of death. And the Bible tells us that the risen Jesus will return as the ultimate king—one who will both judge the world and save God's people.

Exile (Psalm 137): Throughout their history, despite all God had done for them, the people of Israel disobeyed the law and neglected their special relationship with God. Even the kings forgot about God. The very people through whom God planned to bring blessing to the world were thinking, "We know better, God—we'll do things our way". Sound familiar? The rebellion of Adam and Eve was being repeated down through the ages on a massive scale.

Once again, God didn't turn a blind eye to the rebellion of his people. He responded in judgement by taking them out of their promised land. Powerful nations rose up and conquered Israel, and God sent his people away to the surrounding nations. While they were in exile the people were in anguish, because it seemed that God's promises to Abraham were being undone. But even in the midst of bringing judgement (which Israel deserved), God didn't give up on his people or his promises. He preserved a remnant of his people and brought them back into the promised land after 70 years in exile.

Prophets (Jeremiah 31:31-33 and Isaiah 53): Before, during, and after the exile, God sent prophets—spokesmen whose job was to bring God's message to his people. God spoke through these prophets to call the people of Israel back to their special relationship with him, and to remind Israel of the promises he had made. The prophets frequently pointed out the reality of Israel's sin, and warned the people that they were facing God's judgement because of their actions. But the prophets also comforted the people, telling them that God would not forget his pledge, and pointing forward to its ultimate fulfilment. Perhaps most importantly, the prophets looked forward to the coming of a special individual who would lead God's people perfectly and save them from their sin. Which brings us to the New Testament...

Jesus' life (Matthew, Mark, Luke and John): God kept his pledge by sending his Son Jesus into the world. Jesus was an Israelite, a direct descendant of Abraham and of King David. He lived the life of special relationship with God that all of Israel was supposed to live, and he fulfilled the words of the prophets. Unlike everyone before and after him, Jesus never disobeyed God.

During Jesus' life on earth, he preached the coming of the kingdom of God and said it was time for people to be reconciled to God. He did things that showed he possessed all of God's power—things like healing the sick, stopping mighty storms with a word, and even raising the dead. He claimed to have the authority to forgive sins, which his friends and enemies both knew belonged to God alone. He taught things about God with an authority that no-one had ever heard before.

Jesus didn't claim to simply be a good teacher or a kindly worker of miracles. He repeatedly claimed to be God in the flesh—the one whom the Old Testament had promised would come to save God's people. Some were drawn to Jesus, following him closely and trusting him. Others were interested, but kept Jesus at arm's length. Still others—most shockingly of all, a number of Israel's religious leaders of the day—hated Jesus and his message. They saw him as a blasphemer and a threat to their authority, and they plotted to get rid of him.

Jesus' death (John 3:16-17 and Romans 5:6-8): If the subject of a biography has died, their death is sure to rate a mention in the book—maybe as an unexpected tragedy, or simply as the end of their life and their achievements. Yet in all the many biographies I've read, there's one thing I've never seen: the idea that the central figure of the story came into the world *in order to* die. Death is the end of life, but it's not the purpose of life.

Yet incredibly, all four biographies of Jesus present his death in exactly this way—as the very purpose of his life. Jesus himself predicts his coming death before it happens, and clearly sees it as being central to his mission. And Matthew, Mark, Luke and John each devote an enormous amount of space to describing his death and the events leading up to it.

Why?

The Bible's picture is that when Jesus died, he was willingly taking on himself the punishment due to humanity for their rejection of God. Because he lived a perfect life, Jesus didn't deserve death. Yet he willingly chose to go to the cross for us, in our place. Now, everyone who confesses their rebellion against God, admits their need for forgiveness, and turns towards Jesus in trust, can be forgiven and restored into a right relationship with God. One verse in the New Testament puts it this way: "Christ died for sins once for all, the righteous [Jesus] for the unrighteous [all of us], to bring you to God" (1 Peter 3:18, NIV1984).

To put it another way: the essence of sin is humanity putting themselves in God's place, and the essence of salvation is God putting himself in humanity's place. At the cross of Jesus, God acts as our Saviour. God planned the self-sacrificial death of Jesus to demonstrate his extraordinary love for his people, to save them from their sins, and to transform them into a people for himself.

Jesus' resurrection (Matthew 28 and John 20): You'll notice something else when you read biographies:

death is *always* the end of the story. Sure, someone's legacy might live on through their children or their achievements. But their own story is over.

Not for Jesus.

The early Christians made the extraordinary claim that although Jesus actually died, three days later he was physically alive again. The Bible records the testimony of the first eyewitnesses to this incredible event, and the ways in which this message gave rise to the Christian church. When God raised Jesus from death, he was showing that the penalty for sin had been paid and that the world could now be reconciled to God. Adam and Eve rebelled. Israel rebelled. But Jesus Christ, the righteous one, became the saving Lord and the Ruler of God's kingdom. Death could not hold him down.

Jesus' resurrection shows that his incredible claims about himself were true. But it shows much more than that, too. It shows that God has appointed him as the Judge and Ruler over all of creation, the one to whom we all owe ultimate allegiance. The resurrection shows that now is the time for salvation—the time for sinners to turn back to Jesus and find the forgiveness they need by trusting him.

Pentecost and the early church (Acts 2): When Jesus returned to God, he sent the Holy Spirit to live in his followers. Jesus calls the Holy Spirit "the Spirit of truth" (John 14:17) and tells us that the Spirit makes Jesus known to his people, convicts the world of its sin, and comforts believers with the knowledge of God. The Holy Spirit was first given during a religious festival called 'Pentecost', when a group of believers saw something that looked like tongues of fire descend on them from heaven. They began to speak in different languages, and 3000 people in Jerusalem heard the news of the risen Christ and believed. God's pledge to Abraham—that he would provide a blessing to all nations—was being fulfilled as people from all nations became part of God's kingdom. Today, the Holy Spirit empowers followers of Jesus to live in joyful obedience to God and to love and serve others in every aspect of their lives.

Jesus' return (1 Thessalonians 5:1-11): We've now entered the realm of things that God has promised, but which have not yet been fulfilled. The Bible promises that just as Jesus came to earth once, he will come again. But in some ways his second coming will be very different from his first coming. Next time, Jesus will come not as a baby in a manger but as a powerful and glorious king. At that time, he will judge the whole world and punish ongoing rejection of God, wherever it's found. The wonderful news is that everyone who trusts in Jesus will be saved from God's judgement and will be with God forever. Until Jesus returns, God's people are to live in a manner worthy of the kingdom of God. The New Testament is packed with guidance and instructions on what it looks like to live transformed, holy lives as we follow Jesus until he comes again.

The new creation (Revelation 21-22): After Jesus' return, God will make a new heaven and a new earth that will last forever. This can be thought of as the ultimate 'promised land'. Death and pain will be destroyed. Sin and all its effects will be removed. God will dwell with his people in perfect relationship, with his people ruling the new creation under him. The picture language of the book of Revelation tells us of Jesus, "the Lamb who was slain", who will be enthroned alongside God the Father and worshipped by the great multitude of people that he has rescued. This new creation will be the final fulfilment of all God's promises in the Bible, the ultimate hope of

God's people, and the ultimate home of righteousness with Jesus at the centre.

Summary

So there's our overview of the Bible—a story that moves from problem (our rebellion against God) to solution (the death and resurrection of Jesus for us); or from promise to fulfilment. As the Bible shows, the God at the heart of the universe is not just infinitely powerful and righteous, but also infinitely loving, good and gracious. He has gone to extraordinary lengths to save us from our sin—even giving his own precious Son as the rescuer we desperately need.

This is the essence of why the Bible has had such a phenomenal impact on our world, and on so many millions of lives. It introduces us to the God who is really there, tells us how he has designed us to live in his world, and shows us that—in his extraordinary love for us—God has made it possible for us to know him personally and live in a restored, loving relationship with him. Whatever your aims as you embark on reading the Bible, keep in mind that you're reading the greatest story ever told: the story of the God who saves.

4. HOW TO READ THE BIBLE

With all that in mind, it's time for some suggestions to get you started on the adventure of reading this life-changing book for yourself.

If you're just starting out (or even if you've had some experience), reading the Bible can be a daunting task, and we might even be drawn into thinking this is a spooky or mysterious exercise. But the truth is that reading the Bible is, in many ways, a surprisingly straightforward task where we can apply the ordinary rules of reading and comprehension. So with that in mind, here are a few tips—firstly, on how *not* to read the Bible.

Don't read your Bible...

- **randomly:** Avoid opening a page at random, scanning a few verses, finding something that sounds vaguely wise and helpful, and then walking around all day pondering those verses to try and find a personal message from God. You'll probably miss the bigger picture, you'll take ideas out of context, and you might be so distracted that you burn the dinner or crash the car.

- **with fear:** Don't be daunted by the size of the Bible or the magnitude of its message. Take it slowly, one step at a time. As the saying goes, "How do you eat an elephant? One slice at a time!" Don't let the size of the task overwhelm or paralyse you.

- **with yourself at the centre:** Because the Bible is a personal book, it's tempting to look for ourselves (or something relevant to the immediate circumstances of our own lives) on every page. But remember, God (not you or me) is the one at the centre of this story.

- **with scissors and a red pen:** On first reading (or second, or third, or fourth reading), it's tempting to remove or ignore the parts of the Bible we don't like. But (as we'll discuss more in a minute) we shouldn't be surprised when the Bible confronts or challenges us. Don't be quick to dismiss the Bible when it sounds strange to your modern ears.

So then, how *should* we read the Bible? Here are six simple ideas to get you started.

1. With a plan

First, if you don't already have one, get yourself a readable, modern translation of the Bible (if someone gave you this booklet and it didn't come with a Bible, tap them on the shoulder!). The New International Version (NIV) or English Standard Version (ESV) should serve you well.[7]

Next, it helps to have some idea of where to start. There's nothing wrong with starting at Genesis and working your way through to Revelation. Just be aware that this will take lots of time and patience, and you're likely to encounter some concepts that won't make much sense the first time through. If

---

7   There are numerous English translations of the Bible, mostly because different translations have different aims. Some aim to be very literal, providing a word-for-word translation (e.g. the New American Standard Bible). Others paraphrase the original wording to make things easier to understand (e.g. children's Bibles, the Good News Bible, and the Contemporary English Version). For most adult readers, a translation that strikes a balance of readability and careful translation (like the NIV or the ESV) is best.

that doesn't faze you, and you want the satisfaction of reading the Bible from start to finish, go for it.

However, it makes sense to be a bit more targeted in your initial reading. My suggestion is to start with one of the biographies of Jesus' life–specifically, with Mark's Gospel. Mark is the shortest of the four biographies of Jesus, and gives a wonderful introduction to his life and death. And if, as we've already seen, Jesus is the central figure of the whole Bible, it makes sense to start by becoming familiar with his life. It might even be worth reading all of Mark in one sitting (it's shorter than you might think) before then going back and reading it more slowly, one chapter at a time. As you start your slower reading, resist the temptation to rush. Take the time to deeply consider what you're reading, make a note of any questions you have or anything that stands out to you, and ponder what it all means for you and your life. And keep an eye out for answers to these two questions:

- Who is Jesus (especially in chapters 1-8)?
- What did Jesus come to do (especially from chapter 9 onwards)?

After you've finished Mark, here's a simple reading plan for your next few books.

Romans *or* Ephesians

Romans, in the New Testament, is a letter written by Paul (one of Jesus' first followers and a leader in the early church) to the Christians in Rome, and it's the most in-depth letter in the New Testament. Over the course of 16 breathtaking chapters, it lays out the incredible scope of what God has done for us in Jesus. Romans is a book that really needs to be read slowly and thoughtfully, but it will repay this effort by giving you a clear picture of God's extraordinary plan of salvation, culminating in Jesus. If you find Romans a bit daunting, or you're looking for a shorter introduction to Paul's writings, try Ephesians—a six-chapter letter from Paul to the church in Ephesus, covering what God has done for us and what it means to follow Jesus in all areas of life.

Genesis

Genesis is the first book of the Bible. It details God's creation of the world, humanity's fall into sin and our descent into full-fledged rebellion against God, and God's pledge to save humanity and bring blessing to Abraham and his descendants. It's written by Moses, the leader of God's people during the exodus from Egypt. At 50 chapters, Genesis is fairly long, and some parts will be hard work. But it will give you a taste for reading the Old Testament, as well as introducing you to some key themes that become really important in the rest of the Bible (like creation, sin, and God's promises). After finishing Genesis, you could move on to Exodus–the story of God rescuing his people from slavery in Egypt and God instructing the nation of Israel on how to live as his saved people.

Acts

Acts is a short and extremely readable history of the early church in the years immediately after Jesus' death and resurrection. It is written by Luke (a doctor, historian and early Christian), and is effectively volume 2 of the Gospel that bears Luke's name. It covers the period from around 33-64 AD, and shows how Jesus' earliest followers proclaimed the good news of forgiveness and new life that was available through Jesus, and how the early believers began to form themselves into communities called 'churches'. Despite opposition from most of the ruling authorities of the day, the Christian movement grew rapidly throughout most of the known world among both Jews (descendants of Abraham) and Gentiles (non-Jews). Acts is the gripping account of how this happened.

John

Written by John, one of Jesus' closest friends and earliest followers, the Gospel of John is a biography of Jesus, but with quite a different feel than Mark's Gospel. Near the end of his book, John offers this summary of why he's written: "These [things] are written so that you may believe that Jesus is the Christ, the Son of God, and that by believing you may have life in his name" (John 20:31). Perhaps more clearly than any other book, John's account intro-duces us to Jesus as the 'God-man'—both fully human and fully divine. The Jesus you'll meet in the pages of John's Gospel is bold, compassionate, authoritative, gracious, wise, powerful and infinitely loving.

Psalms

Many of the best known and most loved parts of the Bible are found in the book of Psalms, a collection of 150 poems or songs in the Old Testament. The psalms cover a huge range of topics and emotions, including songs of praise and worship to God, sorrow over sin, delight in God's word, lament in the face of suffering, and expressions of trust in God even during the darkest times. Psalms are quoted often in the New Testament, and many of their themes and ideas are directly fulfilled in the coming of Jesus. The suggested reading plan at the end of this booklet will help you discover some 'highlights' from among the psalms.

2. With a partner

If you're reading the Bible for the first time, it makes a lot of sense to do it with the guidance of someone who's had a bit more experience thinking about it. Why not ask a trusted Christian friend to meet up with you once a week over coffee to chat about what you're reading in Mark?[8] Maybe you could read a few chapters of Mark on your own, make a note of any questions you have, then meet with a friend to talk it all through. Or you could ask your friend to

---

8   If you don't know anybody you think could help you, contact the publisher of this book and they might be able to put you in touch with an appropriate contact in a local church.

find some basic Bible study material that will help to guide your discussion.

Of course, there's nothing wrong with reading the Bible on your own. But because there are so many big, potentially life-changing ideas contained in its pages, most people find that it helps to have a friend that they can kick ideas around with and ask questions. Find someone you trust who can pray for you and be a source of guidance and support as you embark on reading the Bible.

3. With patience and perseverance

We might as well admit it: plenty of material in the Bible sounds strange to our modern ears. If you're reading it for the first time, there will be people and places you've never heard of and stories that don't make complete sense at first glance. And if we're honest, it's more than that. The Bible doesn't just sound unusual; it sometimes sounds wrong. It contains ideas that, on first reading, may seem bizarre and even offensive to our modern ears. Indeed, every culture in our world today—and every culture down through history—has found some part of the Bible objectionable.

But when that happens, it helps to keep a few concepts in mind. First, not everything *described* by the Bible is *condoned* by the Bible. Second, it's important to know that some of the instructions given to Israel in the Old Testament don't apply directly to God's people today. With the coming of Jesus, God has introduced a new covenant—one where his people are gathered as his 'church' all around the world, rather than being brought together as a single nation. This means that certain Old Testament laws— while good and right in their time, and important in helping Israel to live as God's holy people—aren't in force among God's people today.

But third, and probably most importantly, we should *expect* the Bible to challenge our preferences and our preconceived ideas. Think of it this way: any meaningful human relationship will involve give and take, the open exchange of ideas, and occasional differences of opinion. If you're close to someone and you never disagree, it means either one of you has stopped thinking, or you're just not talking enough! We disagree with each other because nobody's perfect, and we all have much to learn.

If our human relationships involve this kind of interaction, why would our relationship with God be any different? We live in a fallen world, and we're all far from perfect. We've lost touch with the way God designed his world and how he wants us to live. So why would it come as a surprise that our perfect, righteous, loving Creator challenges our view of reality and points out where things have gone wrong? Why would God simply stroke our egos and leave us to make all the big decisions based on our own opinions? A god who always agrees with us—or who can be conveniently ignored whenever that god's opinion disagrees with ours—is no god at all.

So if you're looking for a book to tell you "Everything is awesome, including you", I have some bad news: the Bible is sure to disappoint. But if you're willing to be challenged—if you're ready to consider what the Creator has to say about you, about the meaning of life, and about the state of his world, even when it's hard to hear—then the Bible is for you. And thankfully, the Bible does so much more than simply challenge and confront. As we persevere with this extraordinary book, we also come to see that despite all our problems the God at the heart of the universe actually loves us, cares for us, and has gone to great lengths to rescue us and save this broken world.

So with all that in mind, be patient as you read the Bible. If things don't make sense straight away, keep going! Persevere. Be willing to think, to have your preconceptions challenged, and even to change your mind. Keep focused on the big picture, rather than always getting distracted by the details. It might also help to have some simple questions in your back pocket. As you read each part of the Bible, ask yourself:

- What does this teach me about God?
- What do I learn about myself?
- How does this prepare the way for Jesus, or what does it show me about Jesus?
- How does this part of the Bible fit into the big picture that centres on Jesus?

4. With personal reflection

Maybe you're interested in reading the Bible because you'd like to be a more informed citizen. You recognize the Bible's historical significance, and you figure that reading some of it will allow you to better understand your cultural heritage or be a more interesting guest at dinner parties. And all of that makes good sense.

As we've already seen, the Bible has made a bigger impact on our world than any other book.

But if that's as far as we go, we'll miss what matters most. The Bible does much more than address governments, nations, cultures and institutions. It addresses each one of us. It speaks to me, and it speaks to you. It comes to each one of us as a highly personal word from our Creator, telling us who we are, what our lives are about, what's gone wrong for each one of us, how we can be saved, and what shape our lives should take now. It's hard to imagine anything more personal!

By all means, read the Bible with an eye on its cultural impact, but be ready to go further. Keep an attitude of personal reflection and openness as you read.

5. With practical common sense

Dealing with 'holy books' that discuss the meaning of Life, The Universe and Everything can feel very unusual. After all, the Bible isn't just an airport thriller to be thrown in the trash when you're done. This is a book about God! Because of that, we might feel as though we need to reach some state of heightened spiritual consciousness before we can really 'get it'. We might think there is some secret initiation required, or some magical technique to be unlocked, before the Bible will hand over its secrets.

But we don't need to approach the Bible with this kind of uncertainty or trepidation. Yes, reading the Bible is a spiritual activity, and it's right to pray for God-given insight (see below). But God hasn't revealed himself through a series of spooky, mystical writings. In his kindness, he has revealed himself in ordinary, plain language that (with a bit of effort and attention) we can all understand.

As you read the Bible and seek to understand it, simply use the normal tools of reading and comprehension that you would use as you read anything. What do the words mean? What event is being described? What is the writer trying to say? How does the previous paragraph help me to make sense of this one? What is the logical flow of ideas? What is the overall argument of the book? These and similarly unremarkable questions are the key to understanding the Bible.

Basically, if you know how to read, you can read the Bible.

6. With prayer

If you're just starting out at reading the Bible and exploring what you believe about God, you might not feel ready to pray. That's understandable. But the Bible describes a God who loves to hear from people who are genuinely seeking him. Why not try saying to God, with as much openness and honesty as you can muster, something like this: "God, I want to know the truth about you. If you're there, and if the Bible is true, please help me to see the truth about you and get to know you personally as I read this book."

That doesn't mean God will instantly zap you with the magical ability to understand everything. It still takes time, and God will usually answer a prayer like the one above through everyday things like our effort and our thoughtfulness, and perhaps the help of a friend. But when we pray for God's help, we're acknowledging that reading the Bible is more than an intellectual exercise. Something much bigger is at stake.

Remember, the Bible is not a safe, easy book. But books don't change the world by being safe and easy! Reading the Bible is demanding, but it is certainly worth the effort. It has the potential to open stunning new horizons on who God is, what life is really all about, why we're here, and how Jesus offers us the hope we so desperately seek. Reading the Bible just might change your life.

Over to you...

APPENDIX A: WHY BOTHER WITH THE BIBLE?

There's no doubt that, in many people's minds, the Bible's reputation has taken something of a battering in recent years. A number of outspoken critics have dismissed the Bible as unreliable and therefore unimportant. Just listening to the sound bites might leave us feeling like the Bible belongs to gullible fools and should be ignored by enlightened, critical thinkers.

But do those claims fit with the facts? Is the Bible really as unreliable as many people claim? Or is it possible to continue studying the Bible without switching off your brain and taking a giant leap of 'blind faith'?

Thankfully, and wonderfully, the Bible is far more credible and reliable than many modern commentators would lead us to believe. In fact, the accumulated weight of scholarly evidence tells us that the Bible is more than reliable; it is so well supported by the weight of history and archaeology that it positively demands our attention.

For our purposes, let's focus our attention on the New Testament. There are really two questions to answer:

- First, is the New Testament in my Bible the same as the New Testament that was originally written back in the first century?
- Second, is that original New Testament (and therefore my New Testament) an accurate record of the events it claims to describe?

Let's tackle the first question: Has the New Testament been accurately passed down to us throughout the centuries, or has it been corrupted—either through some kind of Chinese-whispers-style confusion or perhaps through a deliberate plot to distort the truth?

Historians usually begin to answer this type of question with something called the *bibliographical* test, which asks: since we don't have the original documents,[9] how many copies are there, how reliable and accurate are those copies, and what is the time gap between the originals and the earliest copies? These questions are vital to the work of ancient historians, because no original manuscript of any work of ancient literature has survived.

To get our heads around this question, let's start with another ancient text–one that represents the gold standard in historical reliability: Homer's *Iliad* (written around the 8th century BC).

- There are 643 surviving manuscripts of the *Iliad*, a massive number by any normal standard (e.g. there are ten manuscripts for Caesar's *Gallic Wars* and 20 manuscripts for Tacitus' *Annals*). More manuscripts mean more opportunities to compare copies and confirm that the original has been faithfully transmitted.
- The oldest surviving copy of part of the *Iliad* currently known is dated to within 500 years of the original (again, this is excellent–the average time span between originals and their earliest copies is more than 1000 years).

---

9 That is, the actual books or letters originally written by the hand of Matthew, Mark, Luke, and so on (the technical name for these documents is 'autographs').

Shorter time periods mean less opportunity for the original to be altered.

- The first complete copy of the *Iliad* dates from the 10th century (more than 1600 years after Homer wrote his work).

If that's the gold standard in ancient history, what do we find when we turn to the New Testament?

- There are more than 5600 surviving manuscripts of the New Testament—in Greek alone! If we include ancient copies in other languages (like Latin), the number skyrockets to more than 24 000.

- The oldest surviving copy of part of the New Testament currently known is a small fragment of John's biography of Jesus (originally written between 70 and 95 AD) from the first half of the second century. This means the time gap between this copy and the original is less than 100 years (quite possibly less than 50 years).

- Copies of whole books of the New Testament appear within 100 years of the originals; copies of the entire New Testament are dated to within 250 years of its completion.

Yes, you read all those numbers correctly. On any measure, the New Testament passes the bibliographical test with flying colours. Actually, that's a major understatement. The New Testament sets the standard and raises the bar, dwarfing the statistics for even the best-attested work of ancient literature. Sir Frederic Kenyon, director and principal librarian of the British Museum and an international authority on ancient manuscripts, said, "The last foundation for any doubt that the Scriptures have come down to us substantially as they were written has now been removed".[10]

What does that all mean? It means that as you read your New Testament, you can have the highest possible level of confidence that what you're reading is what the authors originally wrote.

This leaves us with our second question: Just because the original writings have been accurately passed down doesn't mean they're true. So is the New Testament a reliable record of what really happened? Were the original writers telling the truth?

To begin answering this question, we turn to other areas of ancient historical analysis—and our confidence in the Bible only grows. For starters,

---

10 Quoted in FF Bruce, *The New Testament Documents: Are they reliable?*, Eerdmans, Grand Rapids, 2003, p. 15.

the New Testament passes what is often called the 'internal' test, which examines the internal consistency of a document (or a series of documents). Across 27 diverse writings, we find complete agreement on every main point, and on all significant details that support those main points. Where minor discrepancies have been alleged, the vast majority of these supposed discrepancies have been explained through careful historical analysis and basic principles of interpretation.

It's worth pausing to look at one example. Let's examine two different accounts of the death of Judas Iscariot, the man who famously betrayed Jesus to the Roman authorities for 30 pieces of silver. Matthew's account tells us that Judas, filled with despair at his mistake...

> ...threw the money into the temple and left. Then he went away and hanged himself. (Matthew 27:5, NIV2011)

Luke (the author of Luke and Acts) gives us this vivid piece of testimony:

> With the payment he received for his wickedness, Judas bought a field; there he fell headlong, his body burst open and all his intestines spilled out. (Acts 1:18, NIV2011)

So which is it? Did Judas give the money away, or use it to buy a field? And did he die by hanging, or as the result of a fatal fall? On first glance, we have a problem.

But when we look a little more closely, the issue is easily resolved. Let's start by reading the next two verses of Matthew's account:[11]

> The chief priests picked up the coins and said, "It is against the law to put this into the treasury, since it is blood money". So they decided to use the money to buy the potter's field as a burial place for foreigners. (Matthew 27:6-7, NIV2011)

Do you see how these two accounts can now be harmonized quite simply? A sorrowful Judas returns his "blood money"; the chief priests use the money to buy the potter's field; Judas hangs himself in this field; after he dies, his body falls from the noose and he meets his (fairly graphic) final fate. We're reading two separate yet complementary accounts of the same event. And rather than presenting us with a problem, we're left with increased confidence that

---

11 Remember footnote 5 (in chapter 2) on the importance of context.

we're reading real history, not a conspiracy among religious fanatics who have cooked the books. The same kind of process can be applied to many other examples, yielding the same outcome—an assurance that we're reading a truthful historical record, the work of real people in real times and places.

The New Testament also aces the 'external evidence' test, which looks for ancient literature or other evidence that confirms the document in question. A raft of non-Christian historians—most notably Josephus, Pliny, Tacitus, and Thallus—combine to confirm important details of the New Testament. The writings of early Christians further confirm this picture. In fact, even if we had no manuscript copies of the New Testament itself, most of the New Testament could be reconstructed solely from quotations present in the writings of early Christians.

What else gives us confidence that the New Testament is reliable? For one thing, it's written by eyewitnesses who wrote within just a couple of decades of Jesus' own lifetime. That makes it really hard to make up stories like the resurrection. I mean, if I wanted to convince you that a friend of mine had died and come back to life about 20 years ago, and that more than 500 people had seen my friend in his resurrected state (which is exactly what Paul claims about Jesus in 1 Corinthians 15:3-6), and if most of those 500 people were still alive today, what would you do? You'd track down some of those eyewitnesses and demand confirmation of my story. And if lots of them said, "Nope, that never happened—your friend's pulling your leg, or he's crazy", it's unlikely that my fanciful little tale would revolutionize the ancient world and span the globe 2000 years later.

What's more, the New Testament writers didn't have a huge incentive to invent their stories about Jesus. For one thing, a lot of the stories make them look personally bad. Jesus' earliest followers are often shown as being dimwitted, stubborn, and sometimes unhelpful or even hostile towards Jesus (Paul, one of the earliest converts to Christianity, spent his pre-Christian days imprisoning and murdering believers!). What's more, their testimony brought dire personal consequences. All of the New Testament authors (as well as countless other early Christians) were arrested, imprisoned, or even killed for their claims about Jesus. If it were all a lie, what would have happened? Sure, maybe a few zealots would have stayed the course and refused to recant—but all of them?

Overall, then, we have a mountain of good evidence that assures us our New Testament is an historically reliable and trustworthy record of real events.

Hopefully this brief overview has given you an insight into why Christians trust the Bible. But to properly understand why we should bother with this book, there's one more idea we need to understand. It's a claim that goes way beyond historical reliability and brings the Bible right up into our personal space.

The Christian claim is that the Bible is inspired by God and is a direct revelation from God.

That's right. The Bible claims to be more than just a history book or a handy guide to spiritual living. It claims to be a message *from* God. As we read the words of the Bible, we are reading the very words of our Creator.

This doesn't mean the Bible came from heaven like an email from God that the human authors simply forwarded to us. The personality and style of each author shines through, and the human role in the Bible's authorship is important. But as the human authors wrote, God 'carried them along' or 'inspired' them in such a way that their message was (and is) God's message (see 2 Peter 1:21).

The Bible itself claims to be "breathed out by God" (2 Timothy 3:16). That was certainly Jesus' own attitude to the Old Testament as he looked back on it.[12] And the New Testament carries the same weight, having been written by authorized, commissioned spokesmen that Jesus hand-picked to bring his message to the world.

This is a staggering claim, but it's incredibly good news.

Some people assume that God is either not there at all, or simply can't be known. Others believe that God can only be discovered through our intuition, or through the careful application of logic and reason, or perhaps through personal spiritual experiences. But the Christian claim is that God has spoken. As one author famously put it, "He is There, and He is not Silent".[13] In his kindness, God has taken the guesswork out of our desire to know him. He has

---

12 Jesus saw the Old Testament as unbreakable (John 10:35), indestructible (Matthew 5:18), the "commandment of God" (Matthew 15:3), and the "word of God" (Mark 7:13) spoken directly by God (Matthew 22:31).
13 This is the title of a book by Francis Schaeffer (1912-1984), an influential Christian leader in the 20th century.

made himself known by speaking to us clearly and decisively in a way that we can understand, ponder, remember, and share with each other.

By the way, the idea that the Bible is inspired by God is key to understanding how the Bible was originally compiled. There are some fairly spectacular conspiracy theories out there (spectacularly interesting, and spectacularly inaccurate) about how the 'canon'[14] was formed, thanks to the likes of Dan Brown and his novel *The Da Vinci Code*. But amid various theories about politically motivated church councils and Roman Emperors, here's the most important point: when compiling the New Testament, the early Christians never saw themselves as determining which books were 'God's word' and which books weren't. Instead, the early Christians merely recognized and formalized the authority that the God-inspired writings already possessed. As historian FF Bruce says, "When at last a Church Council—the Synod of Hippo in AD 393—listed the twenty-seven books of the New Testament, it did not confer upon them any authority which they did not

---

14 The word 'canon' means something like 'measuring stick', 'standard' or 'index', which is why Christians sometimes refer to the 66 books of the Bible as 'the canon'.

already possess, but simply recorded their previously established canonicity".[15]

Christians have sometimes described this by saying that Scripture is 'self-authenticating'. That's a fancy way of saying that each book of the Bible doesn't *become* God's word when enough people get together and declare it to be so. Each book of the Bible simply *is* God's word; Christians down through the centuries have merely recognized what God has given them.

Let me put it another way: if you're not convinced about the Bible yet, try it and see. Read it. Historical background and evidence are helpful, but the real proof of the pudding is in the eating. As the famous 19th-century pastor Charles Spurgeon once said, "Defend the Bible? I would as soon defend a lion! Unchain it and it will defend itself!"

To sum up, what have we seen? On multiple fronts, the Bible comes to us as an accurate, trustworthy, historically reliable record of real events in ancient history. Indeed, the Bible can stand toe-to-toe with any other writing from the ancient

---

15 FF Bruce, *The Books and the Parchments: How we got our English Bible*, rev. edn, Fleming H Revell Co, Old Tappan, NJ, 1984.

world and more than hold its own. The truth is that other ancient works can only dream of having the kind of evidence that stacks up in favour of the Bible. So you can get on with reading the Bible safe in the knowledge that you're not checking your brain at the front cover. This book has withstood the highest levels of scrutiny that history can muster.

Maybe most incredible of all, the Bible makes the radical claim to be the very word of God. Yet rather than wilting under the pressure of this extraordinary idea, the Bible has continued to flourish and make its presence felt in every culture throughout history. It truly is a book like no other.

APPENDIX B: OVERVIEW OF THE 66 BOOKS

The Old Testament

Style of writing	Books	Think of it as...
Pentateuch (narrative)	The first five books: Genesis Exodus Leviticus Numbers Deuteronomy	The story of God creating the world, humanity rebelling against God, then God responding by choosing a people for himself (the nation of Israel) and graciously saving them.

History (narrative)	Joshua Judges Ruth 1-2 Samuel 1-2 Kings 1-2 Chronicles Ezra Nehemiah Esther	The historical record of God's dealings with the people of Israel from the time they entered the 'promised land' after leaving Egypt (around 1400 BC) through to God's people returning to Jerusalem after a period in exile (around 430 BC).
Poetic and wisdom literature	Job Psalms Proverbs Ecclesiastes Song of Songs Lamentations	Books that cover a huge range of topics, including subjects like: • grappling with suffering • how to live with true wisdom in God's world • the futility of sin and the emptiness of life without God • celebrating and praising God's goodness.

Major prophets	Isaiah Jeremiah Ezekiel Daniel	Messages from God, through his appointed spokesmen, to his people over a period of several hundred years. God reminds Israel that he has saved them, warns them of the consequences of ongoing sin, and promises that he will remain faithful to his promises. He also promises the coming of an anointed king or saviour who will rescue his people once and for all.
Minor prophets	Hosea Joel Amos Obadiah Jonah Micah Nahum Habakkuk Zephaniah Haggai Zechariah Malachi	Similar in content to the major prophets. They're called 'minor' not because they're less important, but simply because they're generally shorter in length.

The New Testament

Style of writing	Books	Think of it as...
Gospels	Matthew Mark Luke John	Biographies of Jesus, covering his birth, life, death and resurrection. Written by eyewitnesses and followers of Jesus.
Acts (narrative)	Acts	A short history of the very early church, in the first few years following Jesus' life, death and resurrection. Written by Luke (it's essentially Luke, volume 2).
Paul's letters	Romans 1-2 Corinthians Galatians Ephesians Philippians Colossians 1-2 Thessalonians 1-2 Timothy Titus Philemon	Letters written by Paul, one of the earliest Christian leaders, to churches and individuals in the first century. Paul's letters explain what Jesus did and highlight the implications for his followers.

General letters	Hebrews James 1-2 Peter 1-3 John Jude	Letters written by other leaders within the early church to individuals and churches. In many ways these are much like Paul's letters, but the individual style of each writer shines through.
Apocalyptic	Revelation	Written by John, this book is filled with vivid and startling imagery. These images combine to provide a unique vantage point on God's sure and certain final victory over death and evil, which will happen when Jesus returns.

APPENDIX C:
A 6-MONTH INTRODUCTORY
READING PLAN

There's enough in this basic reading plan to keep you going for six months (reading five or six chapters a week). Of course, you can pick up the pace and read more, or just focus on the parts that interest you the most. But following this plan will get you started with a great Bible overview.[16]

Week 1	Mark 1-5, Psalm 1
Week 2	Mark 6-10, Psalm 2
Week 3	Mark 11-16

16 For a brief introduction to each of the books in this reading plan, see the information in chapter 4 under '1. With a plan'.

THE BOOK OF BOOKS

Week 4	Romans 1-4, Psalm 8
Week 5	Romans 5-8, Psalm 15
Week 6	Romans 9-12, Psalm 19
Week 7	Romans 13-16, Psalm 23
Week 8	Acts 1-6
Week 9	Acts 7-12
Week 10	Acts 13-18
Week 11	Acts 19-24
Week 12	Acts 25-28, Psalm 40
Week 13	Genesis 1-5, Psalm 42
Week 14	Genesis 6-10, Psalm 46
Week 15	Genesis 11-15, Psalm 51
Week 16	Genesis 16-20, Psalm 73
Week 17	Genesis 21-25, Psalm 90
Week 18	Genesis 26-30, Psalm 95
Week 19	Genesis 31-35, Psalm 96
Week 20	Genesis 36-40, Psalm 110
Week 21	Genesis 41-45, Psalm 118
Week 22	Genesis 46-50, Psalm 139
Week 23	John 1-5
Week 24	John 6-10
Week 25	John 11-15
Week 26	John 16-21

matthiasmedia

Matthias Media is an independent Christian publishing company based in Sydney, Australia. To browse our online catalogue, access samples and free downloads, and find more information about our resources, visit our website:

www.matthiasmedia.com

How to buy our resources

1. Direct from us over the internet:
   – in the US: www.matthiasmedia.com
   – in Australia: www.matthiasmedia.com.au

2. Direct from us by phone: please visit our website for current phone contact information.

3. Through a range of outlets in various parts of the world: visit **www.matthiasmedia.com/contact** for details about recommended retailers in your part of the world, including www.thegoodbook.co.uk in the United Kingdom.

4. Trade enquiries can be addressed to:
   – in the US and Canada: sales@matthiasmedia.com
   – in Australia and the rest of the world: sales@matthiasmedia.com.au

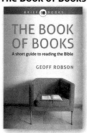
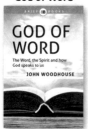

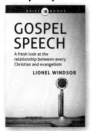

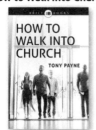